War Time Poetry

Copyright © 2012 by Richard Hampton
All rights reserved.

ISBN-10: 1453860282
EAN-13: 9781453860281

War Time Poetry
Richard Hampton

For my loving family, your unyielding support and love made this possible.

Forward

I was initially inspired to write War Time Poetry as a dedication to the sacrifices of our nation's military; however I am reminded that everyone of us faces our own demons that threaten our lively hood. Many occupations or circumstances can be related to these writings. I believe this because, many of the people that surround us in our day-to-day lives have occupations that take a substantial amount of courage and yet they are hardly recognized. Fire fighters run into burning buildings to rescue strangers. Police officers come to the beck and call of anyone that asks for help. Doctors, nurses, EMT's, paramedics and many other healthcare professionals put their time and effort into improving the quality of life or saving the lives of the people in need. These are but a few examples of people that put their lives on the line and demonstrate courage in the line of duty every day.

Courage is an interesting word that has so many different meanings to people. To some courage is only related to a battlefield. Since 9/11 the men and women of the United States armed forces (active duty, reserve, National Guard and Coast Guard) have placed their lives on the line to protect this great nation from terrorism. These men and women demonstrate courage on a daily basis yet they do not ask for recognition, it is a calling that they answer for their brothers and sisters in arms that please them the most.

Military families also demonstrate a great amount of courage as they support their spouses in their duties, often taking care of the home front for up to 15 months at a time. They also willingly support their spouses and anxiously await their return.

These writings also provide examples of how people that have participated in arduous conditions whether on the battlefield or the home front can ask for help in order to improve their daily lives. It takes courage for someone to ask for help, especially for mental health conditions such as Post Traumatic Stress Disorder (PTSD) or "shell shock" as it was once referred to.

Thank you to my wonderful wife, Julie, who stood by my side and supported me during this endeavor and to my sons, Ricky & James, who helped me to name some of my works.

My brothers and sisters, that guided and protected me during my military career, without you none of this would have been possible. Thank you for your help and service.

Our great nation has valiantly fought a global war on terrorism for almost 10 years. This has claimed the lives of over 6,000 service members and accounted for over 44,000 wounded in action during Operations Iraqi and Enduring Freedom and Operation New Dawn. Our brave men and women of the Armed Forces are paying the ultimate sacrifice for the security of our nation.

During these operations our courageous men and women were exposed to the side of humanity that no one should have to see. But unlike the physical wounds that have received immediate attention and care there is another wound affecting thousands of our brave service members which is an "invisible wound." That wound is Post-Traumatic Stress Disorder (PTSD).

Service members suffering from PTSD are afflicted with mental and emotional scars that can affect their emotional stability, relationships, work-ability, and how they function in society, often resulting in emotional numbness. However, certain situations may "trigger" painful memories which lead to the service member using maladaptive behaviors to cope with an overwhelming change in their emotional state. These reactions can make it difficult at time for people suffering from PTSD to have full, meaningful relationships, maintain stable employment and/or re-integrate into American society.

Responses to triggers will vary from person-to-person and are situational driven. Triggers may present themselves as sounds such as sudden loud bangs or sirens; sights such as injured or dead bodies in a movie or on TV; smells such as gun powder; and situations such as being in large crowds, traffic or having someone standing behind them. These are just examples of triggers that may cause an immediate emotional, mental, and physical reaction for the service member or veteran. Please note that these responses will vary on an individual basis and may manifest themselves as flashbacks, anxiety attacks, avoidance and withdrawal from life and may or may not be visible to others.

Family, friends and significant others can play an important role in supporting their friend and loved one struggling with PTSD. In light of recent recognition of PTSD due to troops returning from deployment resources have become readily available. These resources include books, marriage and couples therapy and the National Alliance for Mental Illness (NAMI.org) to name a few.

People with PTSD can overcome the negative situations or triggers that are associated with a past trauma by obtaining professional psychiatric assistance. Dare to hope for a better and brighter future by seeking assistance, it's never too late to ask for help. Additionally, service members may find assistance through their medical, mental health and deployment health departments, MilitaryOneSource.com and Veterans may also contact their regional or local VA office for assistance.

Wounds

Reminders of the past
Scars that will forever last

Some are obvious while others are hidden

Does size really matter?

Some are superficial
And others run deep

Clothing and make-up may conceal these wounds

Memories are reminders of the past
Memories are often the hardest wound to heal

They may haunt us until our grave

Some fight for God
Some fight for country
Some fight for their loved-ones
They all fight for survival

Some are wealthy
Some are poor
All of the fight in this terrible war

War on terror
But Bin Laden is dead
We've cut off the evil serpents head

So why do continue to fight
When may our troops come home?
Have we not declared victory?

Doom and destruction surrounds us
The devil plays with our minds
And corrupts our heart

Society goes to war to sooth an ego
Young and old lose their lives
While politicians ignore their cries

Surrounded by people
Yet I'm stranded

Trapped in a lonely and desolate place
Filled with darkness

Life feels hopeless
The world is devouring me
Eating away at my mind

Intrusive thoughts are like the plague
Stopping me from functioning
These thoughts are trapped in my mind

I long to be free

To hell with this world
It's a self absorbed rat race
Living is a form of disgrace
If not for the forgiveness and loving of our Lord

Jesus has provided us a gateway
The gateway to eternal life
A life not filled with greed and envy
Paradise awaits those who are faithful

So why do we live a life full of sin
We consume ourselves with lust and greed
With every breath we are closer to our death
Shall our last breath take us to heaven or hell

P.T.S.D.
Memory, tragedy
Fighting, isolating, depressing
Torment, guilt, grief, anger
Loving, caring, accepting
Joyful, hopeful
Free

Depression
Sad, lonely
Crying, debilitating, withdrawing
Disgusted, hopeless, inadequate, fatigue
Smiling, laughing, joking
Joy, ecstatic
Happy

Anger
Primal, displeased
Damaging, stressing, shouting
Harmful, destructive, negative, painful
Relaxing, soothing, satisfying
Peaceful, content
Calm

Deadly hurricane
Strong winds devastate the lands
Death and destruction

Heaven is Divine
Brining peace, beauty, grace and joy
Glory be to God

Bountiful Ocean
Deep Blue Ocean full of life
Mysterious world

Corpsman
Compassionate, brave
Daring, courageous, caring
Saved lives for over 113 years
Doc

Global war on terror, watch out Al Qaeda
Our nation's desires are pacific
You challenged our utopia
Those who fight are patriotic
Harsh conditions
Our troops faced chaos
Added to their perdition
Nothing compares to the feelings of loss
Their souls did not face persecution
Thousands more traumatized forever
They sacrificed on behalf of a grateful nation
Suffering from a combat disorder
Anguish and sadness fuel their emotions
They search for tranquility
Questioning their own mortality, they crave felicity

Patriotism, country over self, that's how it began
Patriotism, is for you and me
Patriotism, is for everyone
Patriotism, must be done
We must stand united
In order to be free
Those who live free are excited
Though we may not always agree
Bold men and women give their life
Sacrifice is common in society
So others may live free of tyranny and strife
It's our nature to be free
Life is precious and enduring
We should spend it rejoicing and not mourning

Death has many faces
Disease, bullets, bombs
They lay waist to society
Destroying everything they touch

They have destroyed so much
Suffering is universal
Pain is plentiful
The world suffers with inhumanity

Revolution abounds
Screams are the sounds
Unrest
Led to protest

Lives will be lost
For this worthy cause
Humanity has paid the cost

Deployed

I'll be gone for up to a year
Missing your warm embrace
Now don't you go and shed a tear
Because your love I can't replace
I held you tight
And kissed you soft
Being with you was my delight
I remember life in our beautiful loft
It was our paradise from the
Freedom was ours at last
Our emotions unfurled
Like a ships mast
Memories have seen me through
For now I can re-united with you

Peace
Harmony, hope
Tolerating, forgiving, loving
Dream for some, reality for others
Joy

Death
Dark, eternal
Grieving, agonizing, haunting
Awaits us all
Final

Depression
Guilt, isolation
Torments, over-whelming, consuming
Nemesis of self-esteem
Agony

Shell shock
Nightmares, flashbacks
Depressing, enraging, intruding
Invisible wound
PTSD

War
Bloody, inhumane
Devastating, killing, unsettling
Some gave all
Atrocity

Anger
Loud, Cruel
Harming, destroys, insulting
Wounds everyone
Rage

Equilibrium
Nature a delicate place
Fights the human race

Happiness and hope
The keys to tranquility
Contribute to peace on earth

Wounds
Personal, painful
Disfiguring traumatizing, piercing
An eternal reminder of war
Torment

War
Clash, struggle
Fighting, bloodshed, hostilities
Wounds us all
Combat

The young and old
The brave and bold
Patrol these hostile lands
All to fit some politicians plans

Suddenly the patrol hit an IED
Gun fire rains in all directions
Screams abound this battlefield

Medics tend to the atrocity caused by the blast
They will forever be haunted of these memories in the past
Blood and limbs litter this field
When will this conflict yield?

Destiny

The dead bodies haunt me
But I don't let these flashbacks bother me
I'm in control of my destiny

I refuse to feel this pain
This pain attacks me in vain
I'm in control of my destiny

This pain no longer messes with me
I have the power of the trinity
I'm in control of my destiny

I'm no longer afraid to close my eyes
These nightmares no longer haunt me
I'm at peace with the past
Those nightmares have passed

I've found freedom and faith in my life
There is no more strife in my life
I'm in control of my destiny

Never Ending Thought

It's dark and scary
The night is haunting
It is full of fear and anxiety

The thought of closing my eyes brings torment to my heart
Memories of the past linger in my thoughts
They terrorize my dreams

The long sweaty nights bring about grief and sorrow
It's a constant battle between reality and the shadows of the past
This trepidation perverts my life and brings about rage and numbness
Reflections of the past will overcast me tomorrow
My life will forever be full of sorrow

The Journey

As the raven perches on the tree
His red eyes glare at me

As I pass him I feel the dark clouds overcome me
His glowing red eyes pierce into my soul
I no longer feel whole

His gaze paralyzed me in time
Even though years have gone by my soul is still tarnished
Every time that I close my eyes
He plagues my dreams with harsh screams and cries

Some years later, I awoke to a glimmer of light that struggled to find its way through the dark clouds that haunted me
Its rays from above
Illuminated a dove
The dove followed me during the final stages of my journey and his gaze brought peace into my soul

His presence gave me hope that my life would no longer be in turmoil

As my journey came to an end my soul was freed of the screams and cries of the past and replaced with hope and happiness

Darkness

My world is dark and full of danger
The frustration builds inside of me
I pray to be able to control the anger

But my prayers seem to go unanswered
Instead my mind is plagued with racing thoughts of the past
My ability to dream has been clouded

This darkness has haunted me for years
I often find myself in tears

My prayers were finally answered
I was able to receive help for these worrisome and pestering nightmares
The healer first had to put me through hell in order for me to see the light
Once I was able to see the light my body and soul were filled with delight

Udari Convoy Crew

Afghan Aid Station

A Warrior's Struggle

A proud warrior was once able to share happiness, joy and love with those around him.

One day he was called upon to engage in battle with a rival nation. During this conflict he experienced anger, hardships and tribulations. The dark cloud of war made him feel unease as he witnessed the fall of his comrades.

Upon returning from this savage war his emotions became more intrusive. Love, joy and happiness were no longer emotions which he could feel. The dark shadow that was cast upon him only allowed for rage, anger, hate and numbness to be felt.

There was now an internal struggle to find his lost emotions that he once held dearly to his heart. One day he happened upon a healer that said, "I can remove this dark shadow from your life and once again allow you to feel peace." The healer informed the warrior that he would need to re-experience some of these horrific events in order to be healed. The warrior agreed to his demands and so began the purging of the demons that haunted him.

After a period of time with the healer the warrior was able to once again experience joy, love and happiness in his life. The shadow that once followed him was removed and he was able to bask in the sunlight once again. He was at peace at last.

Sacrifice

The heroic dead are left on the battle field
They wait for someone to bring them home
But what did their deaths yield?

Did they die so that you could protest?
Did they die for freedom?
Why don't you put on a Kevlar vest?

Do you fear death?
Well rightly so
Many have said "tell them that I love them" with their last gasping breath

Many have felt torment and suffering
Don't allow their sacrifices to be in vain
These warriors' offerings are nothing short of pain

War has casted a dark cloud upon society

Let us not allow our dread to distort the memories of the dead

The Crop

As skies grew dark a fog rolled in overshadowing the farmer's crops. The lack of sunlight caused his crops to reach for the sky. They grew longer in an attempt to take in the suns nourishing rays.

This proved to be unsuccessful and the crops began to slowly wither away. Some crops died while others struggled to survive even though they were wilting away.

As the farmer returned he took notice of this dark cloud over his field of once bountiful crops. He prayed for the darkness to go away.

He then began to fertilize and water his crops that were able to with stand the darkness. Through his persistency and strength the fog and dark clouds began to roll away from his lands. The sun was once again shining brightly upon his crops.

The dark clouds however in the distance waiting patiently to return. But for now peace and prosperity will fill the lands.

The Call

It was a cold and rainy day when a young woman received an unexpected phone call.

Her eyes began to tear and throat began to dry

Death called shattering her innocent life

Three men arrived at her door, one bearing a cross the other two bearing mourn

They bore a message that caused her to feel much remorse, anger and sorrow

She would not be able to see her husband tomorrow

Revenge

The sirens go off
Young and confident men frantically scatter
But will their direction matter?

After the encounter there are feelings of excitement, embarrassment, frustration and sorrow
They will not be able to see their comrades tomorrow
Weary and angered these men prepare for their revenge

Combat loads ready
Weapons held true and steady
Foot-patrols and convoys search out this cowardice enemy
As the old saying goes "an eye for an eye" all these men could see was bloodlust

Politics

All of the strength and training in the world will not allow one to cheat death
Death awaits us all as we take our last breath
Great warriors lose their lives
Only to be survived by lonely and grieving wives

Families are destroyed in the name of democracy
Politicians pervert our country
They're preoccupied with greed

The media feeds the pride of the President
Winner of the Noble Peace Prize for sending more troops to their death
His lust for fame has obscured his vision
Causing trepidation within our nation

Uncle Sam

They sent me to a foreign land to fight for Uncle Sam
These god forsaken countries I could give a damn
Violence surrounds me
When will I be set free?

I left my family behind
Now I'm losing my mind

I witnessed death and destruction
I pray for my resurrection

My family doesn't recognize me
I wish to be set free

Drugs and alcohol helped me during these tuff times
Or so I thought now I'm divorced and drowning in my tears

I pray for the help to get me over these fears
Fate led me to a treatment facility
Now I'm armed to fight this disorder
I no longer care about world order

My concern is to find the emotion that I lost in my mind
I now have control over the flashbacks and nightmares that once haunted me

I know that they will forever be a part of my past
But now I feel peace at last

Death and Politics

I didn't start this pain
My brothers didn't die in vain
Politicians sent us to war
So they could bed a whore

President preaches hope and prosperity
Our country feels angst and agony
Our Soldiers battle for their life
So politicians can cheat on their wife

Our pride and desire to spread democracy
Caused misery and scrutiny in our country
How many more must die?
For us to say "Goodbye"

9/11

9/11 what a horrible day
Terrorism struck the USA
What can we do?

Declare war cries the country
This will keep the rich, richer, and the poor, poorer
How much blood must be shed?

Young and bold and the crazy old shipped overseas
They will certainly bring terrorism to its knees
Will this war ever end?

America must surely win
These terrorists have committed sin
Not sin against "God' but to our country
The sweet land of liberty

Truth be told
No matter how bold
Our struggle against terrorism will never end

Blood Brothers

A shout rang out
Calling for a "Corpsman up"
Now what's up?

Thoughts run through Doc's mind as he runs towards the shout
Someone's in pain and agony no doubt
How many are injured?

Cries for help
Cries of pain
They weren't heard in vain

Doc's on hand
And the Marines are glad
While the Marines take lives
The Doc saves lives

Their relationship lasted over 100 years
During which they shared blood, sweat, and tears

A Marine shouted "Semper Fi do or Die"
Doc subtly replies not on my watch

Loss of Control

The noises are confusing
My emotions are abusing
Tensions build within
I'm coming out of my skin

I wish I was calm
But I feel like a bomb
Ready to explode at any minute
Can I out run the fear within it?

God grant me peace
For I can't control the beast

Hell and Hope

With every step my feet kicked up dust
The smell in the air was that of bloodlust
As I knelt on the ground I was faced with ghastly wounds
Wounds that would last with me
My heart was ripped and emotions shattered
I feared the night because I didn't want to dream
Closing my eye brought fear into my life
I couldn't be the same man for my wife
My life was shattered and my soul stained
These thoughts I tried to contain
Now I struggle in vain
My memories I hope to mend
So my soul won't be condemned

Serenity

I woke up with my lovely wife in my arms
We would sit and eat a bowl of Lucky Charms
Out dogs would comfort us with their unconditional love
We would sit by the pool and admire a dove
The water would ease our mood and sooth our bodies
Our children would return and we would have a party
Joy and happiness fills the air
As the night comes to an end
Our family lies down to bed

Screams

Screams of agony
Screams of plight
Screams that may never see the light

Pains turn to numbness
Screams turn to mumbles
Writhing turns to stillness

This is a somber moment
Perhaps his last chance to repent

Goodbye my friend
You've made it to the end

Dear PTSD,

You have been a constant reminder of a chapter in my life that I would like to close. I am not ashamed of anything that I've had to do, however I don't need a constant reminder of the horrors that I've experienced.

    I look forward to the time that you are no longer in my thoughts or dreams. I've allowed you to negatively impact my life and family for far too long. I will endure and persevere over these challenges. I will conquer you and regain control of my life and destiny.

    The rest of my life will be spent loving my family and the next time I'll see you will be in hell.

Best regards,
The stronger one

My Plight

Afraid to close my eyes
Will the night bring my demise?
Darkness falls
My eyes grow heavy
Dreams flood my memory like a broken levy

Why am I afraid to dream?
My mind wants to scream
Visions from the past
Will this darkness last?

I pray to see the light
All I feel is fright
My heart pounds rapidly, my chest gets tight
Memory escapes me
I'm not here but rather there
There's been a tear in my reality
Is this but a fallacy?

When I awake will I be here or there?
My body doesn't care
The truth must be near

Duality

From the moment of inception
Our world will be full of destruction
Why was I born?

To fulfill some ones fantasy
Of having a family of three
They tore me from the womb
Now I'm sentenced to doom

Is my destiny predetermined?
Must I go to school?
Or may I use a tool
Will I have a wife?
Perhaps I'll learn to kill with a knife

How long do I have to live?
You seem to know everything else
When will the reaper come to claim my soul?
Will it be when I'm collecting cattle?
Or maybe it will be when I'm in battle

Fair well to the Fallen

My bone is in the ground
Dug up by a Blood Hound
Nutrition he must lack
For he's looking for a snack

But my soul will attack
He will be back
Frightened for a few
My duty I must due

My country has taken my family
A flag and some flowers is their prize
That should stop the tears in their eyes

They told them I was a hero
But now I'm a zero
Reduced to bone in the ground
With no one around

Dear democracy thank you for taking my life
Now I'll never be with my wife

Reaper

I once experienced love and happiness
Now all I do is ask for forgiveness
My heart and soul feel numb
At night I want for the reaper to come

Is this fair to my family?
I want the best for my family
But all they see is a shell of me
Can I be there while I wait for the reaper to come?

Deployments have enabled me to feel numbness and isolation
I guess I should feel grateful to my nation
They taught me to accept anger and aggression
Am I the only one that hears voices, experiences hallucinations or hyper-vigilance?

If I ask for help will I be stigmatized?
And my reputation victimized and scrutinized
Friends and family traumatized
Why must so much negativity be associated with me?
For trying to be the old me

Call to War

My country's at war
I knew the call would be near
Eager and sad I pack my bags
Contact is what my mind craves

I thought that leaving my family was the hardest
thing that I'd have to do
From the moment I landed in this country
People try to kill me

Trapped in time
I constantly count the day down
My life has been torn
At times I wish that I was never born

Before battle I reflected on days of old
Just then I began to feel cold
Our clash causes casualties and casts a somberness
For those that we will miss
Some feel a sense of bliss

Joyful that I'm not dead yet
Perhaps I should be upset?
But I agonize over recurring thoughts of death and
destruction

Could of
Should of
Would of
Dwell in my thought
While I'm asleep on a cot

I go home today
Shouldn't I feel happy?
My family is waiting for me
But will they recognize me
My family is excited
Yet I feel isolated

I am home at last
Wishing to come to grips with my past

A King's Tear

There once was a man
Who went to Afghan
He was the envy of the town
After all he was serving the Crown

He was to leave for a year
His wife sheds a tear
Please don't go she pleaded
But the orders of the Crown he heeded

He said his goodbyes with a twinkle in his eyes
Going off to war was his big prize
He slowly boarded the plane with his wife on his hip
After all he was beginning his big trip

Off to War
Was the roar
As the troops boarded the plane
All of the wives and children would remain

Within 24 hours
Some of the ladies were showered with flowers
After the priest paid a visit

These women were enraged and frantic
They were nearing complete panic

Their loved ones had met their demise
Leaving behind their loving wives

For their sacrifice their wives received a flag and
"thank you on behalf of a grateful nation"

Those lucky enough to return from the year -long campaign
They were embraced by their families and an appreciative nation

A.J.

Adjunctive therapy .... Not for me
Adjunctive therapy .... Changed me

In the past I was embarrassed to do art or perform music
I soon became sympathetic
Embracing the arts enable me to explore the ecstasies and excitement
The comfort of my instructors allowed me to become vulnerable and not be humiliated but rather to be stimulated
Reaching out to the arts has brought warmth to my once cold heart

Innocence

Today's young warriors see themselves as bulletproof and invincible

These warriors begin as innocent and eager recruits
But after their training they've been transformed into bruits

Impatient they rush to war
A place they've never seen before

Their innocence has been taken away
They'll never be the same after today

Shocked by the horrors before them
Their souls have been torn apart within them

Anger and aggression mask their fear and torment
These conflicts they've grown to resent

They pray for the day they can get away
However their country says "you must stay"

P.E.

Prolonged exposure ..... How can this possibly help me?
I've spent hundreds of days deployed for my country
Isn't this enough prolonged exposure?
This has caused my mind and body to begin decomposure
I'm tormented by guilt, grief, and anger from the past
I want help but will it last?
The treatment makes me feel so emotional and vulnerable
Talking with my brothers helps me to feel at ease
They help me to deal with my nightmares and flashbacks
I know with their support I won't crack
The therapist puts me through hell
But this treatment will make me well
I must come to peace with the past
If I can't accept the past my agony and angst will last

Treatment may be difficult, but I have the intestinal fortitude to perceiver
My past I will no longer fear
For peace is near
When I leave this place, I'll leave a piece of me in the "quiet room"

My treatment will be successful and I'll no longer feel gloom
My demons are trapped in that room
Prolonged exposure has quieted my demons from the past
Peace is mine at last

A Corpsman's Life

Are you a killer
Or a healer
Demanded the reaper
Life on Earth is so much cheaper

The young man replied I was born to heal
But I'm able to kill
My life is the epitome of duality
Once that first contact is made
I'm not afraid

I can lay down cover fire
Or heal a Marine if I desire
When the call for "Corpsman Up" is bellowed
A Corpsman will run through hell to find this fellow

Life over limb
That's what matters to him
The "Doc" will save as many lives as possible
His will is unstoppable

Some say that he's an angle sent from heaven
To battle hell on Earth
That he was born a special breed
After all most people won't run across a battlefield
to answer a cry for help

The Doc gives freely
As the reaper departed he said "your willingness to sacrifice your life for someone you don't know is completely crazy"
The Doc replied with a gleam in his eye "every person that I save is one less that you can put in a grave!"

A Broken Road Sign

The lack of communication
Across our great nation
Has caused times of turmoil and tribulation

Who's to blame for this break-down?
Surely not our crown
Then perhaps the left wing
Or the right wing

Is it our fault that the bubble burst?
Or was it the banker's greed
Did we live outside of our means?
After all we wanted to be treated like Queens

The desire for a better life has caused much strife
A man can no longer provide for his child and wife

Lack of cooperation and ineffective communication
Will damage our great nation

Ambush

As the farmers moon light the sky
An ambush was near by

Silhouetted by the sky
Many Taliban would die
They were out gunned by those near by

Due to the massive bloodshed of the dead
It caused the sky to appear crimson to the eye

One more battle was won today
But how many more must we slay
In order for us to come home and play

The "Doc"

Death flees from me
It fears my presence

I save lives in every clime and place
I don't discriminate
I liberate

I care for the sick and wounded
Caring for their lives is a must
I've been adorned with this sacred trust

You can find me on land, sea, or air
I am everywhere

The wounded are my flock
I am the one called "Doc"

Rainbow

What's at the end of a rainbow?
On one end I found Iraq
The other Afghanistan
Oh my! Am I a lucky man?

Where was the pot of gold?
It must be the $8 per day
I receive in danger pay

Instead of a warm little leprechaun
These people wish for me to be gone

I am here to bring hope and stability
But now I collect disability

If war is hell then I've been there and back
These countries don't want me back

They want me dead
Or our country's money instead

Perhaps it's the man in me
But I cannot see
What's at the end of the rainbow for me?

Home Alone

My husband's off to war
He's got a 12 month tour
I'm home alone

Mother of three
With a baby to be
I'm home alone

My loved one's gone
I'm about to spawn
I'm home alone

He truly loved his country
He gave his life so we could be free
I'm home alone

Now I'm a mother of four
I'll never see him walk through the door
I'm home alone

Complete at Last

I wish life was neat
Then I'd be complete

My other half is at war
I'm left standing at the door

My thoughts may wonder
But his I ponder

When he's at home
My thoughts will not roam

When will we see each other?
I wish to be with my lover

The love of my life
Will have been removed from strife

When out lips meet
My life will be complete

Love

Love

The love of my life
She is my wife

I love her dearly
I mean this sincerely

My unconditional love
Is as free as a dove

Her picture I adore
Because I'm trapped at war

I long for her embrace
And to see her smiling face

Our fidelity is strong
It will not be long

Our reunion is near
For this is clear

To my surprise
I can see tears in her eyes
This brings me butterflies

As we come together
Like birds of a feather
We shall always be together

Price of War

What is the price of war?
Is it our young?
Perhaps our old
How can we be so bold?

Do we dare take another's life?
With a bullet or a knife

Do we fight over religion?
For there is only one "God", who we all worship in one form or fashion
With varying degrees of compassion

I've yet to meet an atheist in a combat zone
After all we're all just bags of bones

Do we fight over power?
That we so carelessly devour

Perhaps the villain we seek is oil
Yes this is the reason for our turmoil

Our country pays for it at the pump
While our service members pay for it on a "hump"

We've spent billions on this war
Yet we can't feed our poor

Just give us what we want
Then we'll have no one to hunt

We've lost thousands of lives to this war
And destroyed many more
Oh what is the price of this war?

Expectations

Expectations what are they good for?
They mean disappointment for everyone involved

Rigid standards
Stern rules

Attention to detail
How can you fail?

Performance is a must
Decisions must be made

Lives may hang in the balance
Choose wisely
Or someone may die